# *Iowa*

## impressions

photography by Larsh Bristol and Curt Maas

FARCOUNTRY
PRESS

*Right:* Near Ball Town. LARSH K. BRISTOL
*Title page:* Central Iowa sunset. CURT MAAS
*Front cover:* Midseason in the corn field.
CURT MAAS
*Back cover:* A bald eagle hunts for dinner.
LARSH K. BRISTOL

ISBN 1-56037-215-X
Photographs © by Larsh K. Bristol and Curt Maas
© 2002 Farcountry Press

Created, produced, and designed in the United States.
Printed in Korea.
12 11 10 09 08 07 3 4 5 6 7 8

*Above:* Central Iowa. CURT MAAS

*Facing page:* Near Fort Dodge. CURT MAAS

*Above:* Husband-and-wife team Sandy (driving the combine at left) and Scott Grubbs farm near Perry. CURT MAAS

*Facing page:* Hay bales among the alfalfa near Johnston. CURT MAAS

*Facing page:* A muggy summer day ends.  CURT MAAS

*Below:* Early-morning mist.  LARSH K. BRISTOL

*Right:* Beef cattle hard at work preparing for market.

*Left:* The historic Roseman Bridge near Winterset was one of the stars of the movie *The Bridges of Madison County*.  CURT MAAS

*Below:* Threshing oats the old-fangled way at Waukon Days.
LARSH K. BRISTOL

*Right:* Farm partners near McCallsburg.  CURT MAAS

*Below:* Mature pods of soybeans.  CURT MAAS

*Left:* Checking out the soybean crop halfway through the season. CURT MAAS

*Below:* Trying hard to be invisible, a white-tailed deer. LARSH K. BRISTOL

*Left:* Cattail silhouettes. CURT MAAS

*Facing page:* Paint Creek, when its trout residents are resting. LARSH K. BRISTOL

*Right:* Preparing the ground to plant the next round of crops. CURT MAAS

*Below:* Jester County Park near Granger is home to a surviving few of the millions of bison that once roamed Iowa. CURT MAAS

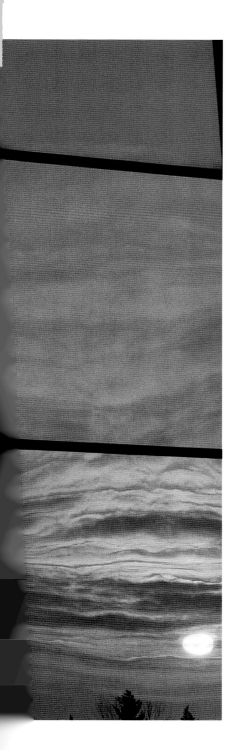

*Left:* Des Moines' Wallace Building reflects some of the Iowa State Capitol's five domes. CURT MAAS

*Below:* Iowa's autumn hardwood colors are brilliant. CURT MAAS

*Right:* Farrier Tim Christopher plies his ancient profession from Bluffton.

*Right:* Future steaks on the hoof, part of Iowa's four percent of the nation's corn-fed beef.

*Right:* Downtown Des Moines stretches along the Des Moines River.
CURT MAAS

*Below:* The Upper Iowa River, near the state's Minnesota border, is fed by trout streams and scenic springs.  LARSH K. BRISTOL

*Above:* Two kinds of golden promises. LARSH K. BRISTOL

*Right:* Heading to work at Decorah's Luther College. LARSH K. BRISTOL

*Above:* Effigy Mounds National Monument covers 1,500 acres and offers 11 miles of hiking trails. LARSH K. BRISTOL

*Left:* Immaculate Conception Church at Harpers Ferry dates from the 1840s. LARSH K. BRISTOL

*Right:* Combining is well on its way by the time the sun wakes up.  CURT MAAS

*Below:* Central Iowa windpower.  CURT MAAS

*Left:* An early–20th century farmstead near Woodward. CURT MAAS

*Below:* Lansing's Commercial Fish Museum tells the story of river fishing and clamming. LARSH K. BRISTOL

*Above:* Corn silk awaits pollination. CURT MAAS

*Right:* Aerial view of Booneville after harvest is in. CURT MAAS

*Left:* Dairy operation near the Mississippi River and Harpers Ferry.
CURT MAAS

*Below:* Harvest bounty at the Seed Savers Exchange, Decorah.
LARSH K. BRISTOL

*Right:* A golden river of corn spills from the combine. <small>CURT MAAS</small>

*Below:* Iowa leads the nation in corn production. <small>CURT MAAS</small>

*Right:* Pride of the pioneer settlers.  LARSH K. BRISTOL

*Facing page:* Scenic limestone bluffs rise above the Upper Iowa River.  LARSH K. BRISTOL

*Right:* Enjoying the autumn afternoon in Yellow River State Forest. LARSH K. BRISTOL

*Below:* Old Fort Madison at the town of Fort Madison reconstructs the frontier post that operated from 1808 to 1813. LARSH K. BRISTOL

*Right:* Remember the thump of uneven sidewalks under bicycle tires? LARSH K. BRISTOL

*Facing page:* Comfortable downtown Waukon. LARSH K. BRISTOL

*Above:* Teaching another generation about the wonders of ice fishing. LARSH K. BRISTOL

*Left:* Winter peace. CURT MAAS

*Left:* Upper Iowa River pleasures.
LARSH K. BRISTOL

*Far left:* Lending a helping hand at a celebration of Native American life at Effigy Mounds National Monument, Marquette. LARSH K. BRISTOL

*Right:* Davenport's signature Centennial Bridge over the Mississippi River. JAMES BLANK

*Below:* Lock and Dam #15 are part of the system that *sometimes* controls the mighty Mississippi. JAMES BLANK

*Above:* More soybeans are produced in Iowa than in any other state. CURT MAAS

*Facing page:* Jack Frost has been busy painting northeast Iowa's trees in autumn colors. CURT MAAS

*Above:* Mississippi wetlands near New Albin. LARSH K. BRISTOL

*Left:* Out for a sleigh ride near Waterville. LARSH K. BRISTOL

*Above:* Stormy central Iowa sundown. CURT MAAS

*Right:* Beast of all burdens. CURT MAAS

*Above:* Are we having fun yet?  LARSH K. BRISTOL

*Left:* A spring storm turns off the sun.  LARSH K. BRISTOL

*Above:* Floating to Des Moines. CURT MAAS

*Right:* The railroad bridge at Fort Madison is the world's longest double-deck swingspan bridge. LARSH K. BRISTOL

*Above:* The best way to enjoy autumn leaves. CURT MAAS

*Facing page:* A young farmer helps wean his family's dairy calves. LARSH K. BRISTOL

*Above:* Quiet patriotism.  CURT MAAS

*Right:* Harvesting soybeans amid corn and beans contours.  CURT MAAS

*Left:* The first blush of autumn. CURT MAAS

*Facing page:* Morning gems
for a garden spider. CURT MAAS

*Left:* Harvest moon, closer than ever.  LARSH K. BRISTOL

*Right:* Rolling road over rolling hills. LARSH K. BRISTOL

*Below:* Looking for the big ones at Lock and Dam #10, Guttenberg. LARSH K. BRISTOL

*Above:* Warm welcome home for the holidays. LARSH K. BRISTOL

*Left:* A whole mile of bridge, at Polk City. CURT MAAS

*Right:* Kayak's-eye view of the Yellow River. LARSH K. BRISTOL

*Below:* Green waves of corn. LARSH K. BRISTOL

*Left:* Getting in the grain. CURT MAAS

## Larsh K. Bristol

Bristol earned a BA in journalism from the University of Wyoming and worked in advertising and photojournalism before returning to his home state of Iowa. He was irresistibly drawn back to the streams, valleys, wooded hills and people of the magnificent Mississippi River Valley. Years as a freelance photographer in the upper Midwest reaffirmed his belief that the light and landscape of Iowa are as magnificent as any in the United States. In August 2006, Larsh Bristol was killed in an automobile accident while traveling one of the rural northeastern Iowa river roads he so loved.

PHOTO: MIKE FLETCHER

## Curt Maas

Originally from Fort Dodge, Maas lived in Iowa most of his life. An honor graduate of Brooks Institute of Photography in Santa Barbara, he traveled the U.S. and the world producing work for a variety of agricultural companies, advertising agencies, and government institutions. His work has been featured in many magazines, documentaries, and books, including *Iowa: Simply Beautiful, Iowa: A Celebration of Land, People, and Purpose,* and *Country U.S.A.: 24 Hours in Rural America.* Curt Maas passed away on September 7, 2005.